Everything's Out in the Open

TERESA TARPLEY

Publisher Published
Radical Women
DBA
PO Box 782
Granbury, TX
76046
www.radicalwomen.com

Radical Women

For those who don't know their true identity or what family they can call theirs, if you're looking to know the deep, dark secrets of your life, I dedicate *Everything's Out in the Open* to you. I'm here to tell you, now is the time to open up the doors and take all that trash to the dumpster where it belongs.

Contents

Acknowledgments

ABOVE ALL, I WANT to acknowledge God. Without His love, grace, and mercy, I would have no story. Had He not saved me from a path of self-destruction and healed my heart, I cannot imagine if I would even be alive.

As I often share, people told me from childhood I had a Joseph anointing on my life and that God was going to use me to save my family. Whether true, I am grateful for those who spoke that over me and continue supporting me in my journey toward Heaven. Thank you for believing in my anointing when I had no clue what that meant.

I thank God for my parents. Despite the wounds they caused and things they might have done better, they gave me life. I learned from them—both what to do and what not to do. In the end, I believe they loved me the best they could. What the devil meant for bad, God used for good. Hmmm. Maybe I do have that Joseph anointing. (See Genesis 50:19-20.)

DNA—something we heard nothing of or had access to as children, changes lives. Because of that technology, I found the truth of my ancestry. I'm grateful for those who pioneered and continued making it available so we can reveal secrets. I owe everything I'm learning about my family to Ancestry.com and the technology of DNA.

Thank you to all my family I'm just now meeting. You accepted me with open arms—sometimes more than those I grew up calling family. I want to let you know I love you, and I thank God for the connections He established once we learned the truth. I'm blessed beyond my imagination at how much love you show me.

For family I don't know yet, I'm looking forward to meeting you. Whether we will form bonds, I don't know, but I'm thankful we have an opportunity we never had before. I look forward to finding more family through research and learning more about those who came before—on Daddy's side, but also Mama's ancestors. With no idea where it may take me, I trust God to make it beautiful, because that's what He does.

Last, I thank my editor and publisher, Radical Women. I could never produce books without Lisa's encouragement and expertise. And thank you most of all, my readers. Without a reader, a book doesn't do anything but sit on a shelf. I pray this book joins my others in changing your life for the better.

Chapter 1~Then and Now

"When I was a child, I spake as a child, I understood as a child, I thought as a child: but when I became a man, I put away childish things."
~Paul the Apostle, 1 Corinthians 13:11 (KJV)

GROWING UP, I WAS told, "What goes on in this house, stays in this house. When grown folks talking, hush. Stay in a child's place."

I didn't know then what I know now. Many families kept a lot of deep, dark secrets. So hidden, I never dreamed the depth they went.

As I got older, I realized those secrets held the key to why I lived much of my life the way I did. I never understood my parents, and they didn't try to understand me.

Throughout my life, people always told me God was gonna use me to save my family. I grew up with this idea, especially after coming out of the darkest time of my life. All the times people spoke those words over me I didn't understand what they meant. Despite spending time in church as a child, I didn't know much about God's salvation, and I sure didn't understand how he could ever use someone like me.

After enduring decades of mistakes and trying to live my way, God got ahold of me, and He saved me. Those words spoken over me, even in childhood, became reality as I moved into ministry.

Now I understand what those words meant. Salvation isn't always about eternity after we die. We live in eternity, and sometimes salvation and God's grace means dealing with things here and now.

Trust me, I didn't feel good about finding out all these deep, dark secrets from my life. I didn't want to believe them, but it was also very exciting to meet family I never knew.

At first, I didn't pay attention to the words coming from an old man, because I had a people addiction. And more than anything, I wanted to break that addiction. When Daddy told me he had 17 kids, I doubted him, believing he exaggerated the truth.

Some people said, "Aww, your daddy ain't got all them kids."

Now that I'm not addicted to people, I wondered whether Daddy told me the truth. Why would he lie about having that many kids?

Imagine my daddy being dead, and I can't talk about this or ask him questions. After his death, I regretted not believing him and asking questions to verify his claims.

Not doing the things I should left strong emotions in the wake, but at the end of the day, I learned to forgive myself. I wish I could have had a close relationship with my biological father. While growing up, I always wanted his last name. Mama never let me use it, and she put a different last name on my birth certificate, which I grew to detest.

As long as I'm living, I'm never too old to do what I want. It might feel hard. What stopped me then can't stop me now. I'm moving forward no matter what.

Half of my life I claimed people as my family, and we weren't even related. Of course, I lied, even had my children thinking we were related to others, but I didn't know my biological family.

After much prayer and healing, I realized another reason I didn't listen to Daddy. I didn't want to be hurt. If he lied about everything, nothing but pain stood ready to greet me. If he told the truth, what would my actual family think? How would they react to the news? Both possibilities scared me. I already covered up years of hurt with sex, drugs, cigarettes. And it took everything in me to break those chains of addiction.

But with these thoughts constantly on my mind, I needed to know the truth. It was time to face reality.

Questions to Challenge You

1. Do you know without a doubt your family biology?

2. Does your family have deep, dark secrets you suspect or know exist?

3. Are you ready to uncover the truth behind any secrets you discover?

Chapter 2~Some Regrets

"*Make the most of your regrets. Never smother your sorrow, but tend and cherish it 'till it comes to have a separate and integral interest. To regret deeply is to live afresh.*"
~Henry David Thoreau

I GREW UP WITH part of my family, but not all. In fact, I had many family members I knew nothing about. In 2013, I connected with some family members.

Before my dad passed, he assured me he had 17 children. Often, when I went to his mechanic shop for a visit, he always asked to let him hold something (meaning he wanted to borrow money), because he had to pay child support.

I remember responding, "I ain't giving you nothing, cause you ain't never done nothing for me."

Or I listened to people who knew him well say, "Yo daddy ain't got all them kids."

Of course, back then I had a people addiction, so although I wanted to believe Daddy, the desire to please people also made me go along with whatever they all said.

Over ten years after my daddy passed, I found out I had a brother. Depression kicked in, because I didn't know if my brother was someone that raped me or maybe someone I dated back in the days before I walked with the Lord. If I had sex with him, oh my goodness. That thought terrified me.

I started getting counseling. Later in life, I regretted not listening to my daddy about his vast number of children. What if he really had 17 kids?

Whenever I saw people, I asked if they knew my daddy. Maybe they had connections to my brothers and sisters. They could know them through my daddy, although I didn't. Growing up, I spent very little time with the man, and he guarded me from many of his connections. I hungered to know more about these possible relatives out of curiosity, but also because I didn't want to date a man only to discover we had the same father.

I even got addicted to watching the *Maury Show* and *Steve Wilkos Show*. Desperate for truth, I thought about trying to become a guest, because I wanted to know my family.

For years, I beat myself up over possibilities of what I might have done in the past. I rebuked myself for not paying attention to what Daddy told me before his death, for not believing his tales of so many children. With him gone, I couldn't go back and ask questions, and that made me mad at myself more than at him.

Eventually, I encouraged myself not to chastise myself so much. I didn't know any better earlier in life, and I couldn't undo any of it.

After I matured in so many ways, I could do better. If I wanted to know the truth and discover blood relatives from my daddy, I could take steps to do it.

As these thoughts played with my mind during the process of counseling, I realized I carried unforgiveness and bitterness toward myself for not listening to my daddy. He hurt me in many ways, and I forgave him, but I had a difficult time forgiving myself. And the time came when I had to deal with that reality. I couldn't change the past, but I could change my actions going forward. And the first thing I needed to change—forgiving myself and letting God heal me.

"If you don't learn from your mistakes, then they become regrets."

John Cena

———✦———

Questions to Challenge You

1. Most people have some regrets. What can you point to in life you regret?

2. Have you forgiven others for their part in the things you regret?

3. Have you forgiven yourself for the things you regret?

Chapter 3~There's No Hidden Place

"For nothing is hidden that will not be made manifest, nor is anything secret that will not be known and come to light."
~Jesus Christ, Luke 8:17 (ESV)

———— ✦ ————

SOCIAL MEDIA EXPOSES A lot of stuff. I mean, a lot. In this day and time, you can't hide much—even if you try.

When I found out I was related to people, I reached out to them, or they reached out to me. Sometimes, it went well, and other times, I left people upset. Fortunately, it no longer matters if someone gets mad at me. God healed me from the addiction to please people.

I feel it's important to know your family—especially if you have 17 blood brothers and sisters. I don't want my daughters and sons dating relatives. As a single woman, I don't want to date a relative. Sad part, that happens a lot. A couple falls in love, even marries, maybe has children together, only to discover a blood relationship. Imagine going through all that.

One day, I called a lady who dealt with the same issues in trying to find her family. We met up, and she hooked me up with a company that could help find close family such as brothers and sisters.

Yes, I took a DNA test. After lots of prayer and consideration. I needed to do it for myself.

I was super excited and called to tell my family that knew my concerns. Everyone was super excited. My decision encouraged others I'm not related to. After I took that giant step, some of them did the same thing.

Of course, whenever you're on the right path, the devil can't stand it. He will do everything to attack, and he poured it on in my life. He went after my emotions and thoughts hard. But in the midst, you gotta keep moving forward. And I refused to walk away in defeat, no matter how much he attacked.

I always think about when I was on crack. Nothing stopped me from doing wrong while I refused to let anything stop me from making positive choices. I am no longer that person, so no matter how difficult it feels, I strive not to do wrong, choosing positive actions instead.

In the midst of waiting on my DNA test results to come back, I woke up one day feeling depressed, because I heard a voice say, "Hot Shot ain't your daddy."

I started crying and praying, but I recognized that sneaky voice. I rebuked the devil. Even though I prayed, I still had a little doubt. I thought about when I asked my mama to take me to see my daddy.

She always told me, "You ain't got no daddy."

Even as a young child, I knew better. Everyone has a daddy. That morning I prayed, begging God to please let Hot Shot be my daddy. I just love the Carpenter family and wanted to prove a biological relationship to them.

Hours passed, and I couldn't stop crying. I called family and other people, crying, asking them if I looked like my daddy.

Everyone I asked responded the same. "You are definitely his child."

They told me I couldn't be denied. Their confidence made me feel a little better, but I still felt a little down and filled with doubts.

A few people I talked to didn't want to hear what I shared. After many of these conversations, I concluded you can't tell everybody everything. Some don't care. Others have their mind on themselves and their issues. And some don't want to hear the truth.

I eventually ask myself, "What are you praying for if you need the opinion of people?"

Needing comfort, I picked up my Bible and read Matthew 17:20-21 (KJV). "And Jesus said unto them, Because of your unbelief: for verily I say unto you, If ye have faith as a grain of mustard seed, ye shall say unto this mountain, Remove hence to yonder place; and it shall remove; and nothing shall be impossible unto you. How-beit this kind goeth not out but by prayer and fasting."

In this passage, the disciples asked Jesus why they couldn't cast demons out of a young boy. They tried their best, but failed. And they didn't understand. These men walked beside Jesus on Earth and had doubts they could do what he sent them out to do.

I knew in my soul I did what God wanted in sending in the DNA, and He already knew the results. Although He welcomed me, I went to people first—perhaps remnants of the people pleasing addiction.

As I read and listened to Holy Spirit, immediately the spirit of doubt and fear left. In all the phone calls and opinions, I wanted other people to confirm my hopes, to assure me I looked like the man I believed fathered me.

God took me to Galatians 1:10. "For do I now persuade men, or God? or do I seek to please men? for if I yet pleased men, I should not be the servant of Christ."

At that moment, I repented of my doubt, seeking for-giveness from God. Then, I praised Him in advance, be-lieving whatever results came back, He promised to bring the hidden things into the light.

I believed the results proved the identity of my daddy.

———— ❊ ————

Questions to Challenge You

1. Have you ever tried to hide the truth from others?

2. How did you feel if someone exposed the truth?

3. If no one exposed the truth, do you fear they might? What can you do with that fear?

Chapter 4~Your Wrong Affected the Child

"As long as you keep secrets and suppress information, you are fundamentally at war with yourself... The critical issue is allowing yourself to know what you know. That takes an enormous amount of courage."

~Bessel A. van der Kolk, The Body Keeps the Score: Brain, Mind, and Body in the Healing of Trauma

---✣---

MANY FAMILIES HAVE VAST amounts of deep, dark secrets. Of course, those hidden truths affect others that had
nothing to do with the events—like your child.

There are a lot of double relations in families. To il-
lustrate, let's say my first cousin, Karen, married Willie,
and they have children. Willie and his family are not my
blood family, but we become extended family. If I married
Willie's son, Craig, and we have children together, our
children will be double related.

Double relations (also known as consanguineous marriage) can cause mental illness and physical diseases.

When blood relatives produce children, genetics come
into play and increase the risk of recessive genes that cause
disease or disabilities. In addition, states within the USA
consider marriage between siblings or half-siblings illegal,
and only about half the states allow first cousins to marry.
Second cousins can legally marry and may carry a lower
risk of genetic issues.

Why risk it?

Sadly, too many people have no clue about all their
blood relatives. Imagine the secrets that put children at
risk without any knowledge.

It's time to stop the foolishness and think about who
you're affecting in the middle of your pleasure. Some people don't think of it like that, but oh well...

God had reasons for instructing us not to have sexu-
al relations with close relatives or relatives of the same

bloodline. (See Leviticus 18.) A lot of times, women blame men for what they did together. Now ladies, some of y'all might have children by two family members, such as an uncle and his nephew.

Of course, not only will your sons be brothers, but they are also cousins. You don't wanna tell one child who his biological dad is because of your guilt and shame for what you did.

What if he gets married and has children, then later they find out they are siblings? Imagine what that does to them individually and as a family. It happens. And with the improving technology of DNA, be sure they will learn the truth.

Now that's deep.

Guess what? Learn to forgive yourself for bad choices and admit to your children the ones you made. It's ok. Don't beat yourself up. You can't undo the past, so let it go.

As long as you're living, you're never too mature. As a side note, age has nothing to do with maturity.

Grow up and tell your children the truth so they don't end up suffering the consequences of your actions. Give them a chance to not accidentally marry a blood relative.

People forgive yourselves, but think about who you affect with every action.

Questions to Challenge You

1. Consider one thing that affected you negatively. Have you forgiven other and yourself for that event?

2. Consider someone you hurt along your journey. Should you seek his or her forgiveness?

3. Be honest: have you forgiven those who hurt you and yourself for wounding the ones you left wounded?

Chapter 5~Child Listen, Pay Attention

"Success in life is founded upon attention to the small things rather than to the large things; to the everyday things nearest to us rather than to the things that are remote and uncommon."
~Booker T. Washington

EVEN THOUGH YOU LISTEN, you can fail to pay attention to the words spoken. And hearing the words doesn't mean you grasped what someone said. Listening and hearing don't always mean the same thing.

Listening involves only a physical process where sound waves hit your ears, and the inner workings translate those sounds into meaningful words. Anyone can listen unless they have deafness. All too often, we can hear, but we put on deafness to avoid the words we don't like.

Hearing often involves more than the physical process. We must open our hearts to the words spoken and let our minds and spirits discern the truth behind what we think we heard.

Not always easy. In fact, hearing can feel impossible at times. And even when we hear clearly, we may choose to ignore what someone told us. I learned that the hard way.

My daddy tried to tell me about all these kids. I listened and maybe heard, but I didn't want to believe what he said.

Honestly, I couldn't hear Daddy, because I was too busy listening to other people. They didn't have a clue what they were talking about. Why, then, did I grasp what they said over what my blood shared with me?

Of course, Mama and others always insisted Daddy was a big liar. I grew up believing that, not knowing him well enough to question what I heard most of my life. Besides, who wants to think their daddy fathered 17 children? Especially when you don't know any of them and didn't grow up in the same house?

At the time he told me these things, I couldn't accept it as truth. I never thought to question others instead of him. Maybe I simply didn't want to believe I really had so many siblings. Maybe I wasn't in the right place to receive that secret. But I needed to hear it—truly hear his words.

Words of encouragement—listen, child. Listen and pay attention to your parents while they are alive. Whether their statements seem possible, get enough information to find out the truth. Once they die, you can't go back and ask questions. They no longer can tell you stories about your family or confirm what you think. Unless they document everything, the past ceases with their last breaths.

Imagine how I felt after Daddy's death. Listening but not hearing or believing, now that he's dead, I wish I could ask him questions and seek the answers as to the truth. I can't, and yes, it left me with regret, which produces emotions I must address now.

If I heard with my heart long ago, perhaps my journey to bring secrets to the light might have been easier.

I can't go back in the past and change anything, so today, I deal with those regrets, forgiving myself and pressing forward. If someone told me to listen with all my heart, it could have saved me many tears.

So, take my advice and pay attention while you can. You may not have tomorrow.

Questions to Challenge You

1. If you could ask your mother or father (living or dead) one question, what would it be?

2. Have you ever sat with a family member and listened to the stories he or she shared?

3. What can you do to learn more about your family ancestry before those who know it leave this earth?

Chapter 6~Withdrawals

"The key for filling the void comes first from knowing God intimately through Jesus Christ, that inborn DNA begging for relationship with our Creator."

~Lisa Bell, Homeless Hearts

❊

HAVE YOU EVER DEALT with an addiction such as drugs, alcohol, cigarettes, sex? Oh yeah, how about being addicted to people? Specifically, the addiction to please people?

I hear your indignation over my suggestion while you think, "Absurd. I've never been addicted to anything!" Remember, we can become addicted to things we never consider addictive. That TV show you can't miss for anything? Food—coffee, chocolate, sugar? I might be getting up in your business right now. Not sorry. Made my point. No judgement from me, for sure.

You name it, we can form an addiction to anything. Most people have some level of addiction, although many of them fall into the non-destructive category. God created us for an addiction to Him, and without filling that hole, we search for an alternative—sometimes to our detriment.

Now I'll climb down from the soapbox and return to the harmful addictions we may need to break. Although, deciding to break any addiction applies. Some of you understand exactly what I mean in the rest of this chapter. I hope many of you don't. But if you want to experience withdrawal, try breaking one of those "habits" you'd never call an addiction.

Dealing with the phase of withdrawals from addiction is excruciating and challenging. It affects both the body and mind. Although the following signs of withdrawal apply to substance abuse, any withdrawal can cause them. Physically, a person may experience sweating/chills, headaches, insomnia, fatigue, loss of appetite, and a host of other ailments during withdrawal. Mentally, some symptoms include mood changes and swings, depression, confusion, poor concentration, and more.

Withdrawal from an addiction—of any kind—requires deep commitment alongside God's grace. The process takes time and the continued desire to break the addiction. In my next book, *Withdrawals*, I visit this subject in greater detail based on my life experiences.

Committed to transparency with my readers, I must admit at the time of writing this chapter, I dealt with a phase of withdrawal from a people pleasing addiction. The need stemmed from being so hard-headed and not listening to my dad when he told me about his 17 kids.

My heart ached over the situation. Perhaps more so because I couldn't go back and seek his forgiveness for desiring the approval of other people over his and God's. Writing peeled back a layer of this addiction, so I had to deal with it before I could continue my journey of life.

I learned from him that when you try to tell a person something, and they don't listen well, you get back. You did your part. You can't control their actions nor their desire or ability to hear the words you have for them. Later, they'll wish they listened and heard.

That was me as I wrote these words.

I wish I listened. Wish I heard what he said. Lament that I didn't follow up, check his claims, or demand more information. As the ancient Scottish proverb claims, "If wishes were horses, beggars would ride."

Instead, I thank God for the healing process. I'm learning to let go of the past and the need to please anyone other than my Lord. I no longer beat myself up—at least most of the time. Sometimes, people must tell me to put down that big stick.

I also realized I can't blame my daddy. For a long time, I carried around anger against him, and I wasn't sure about the root of that anger. While I withdrew from always wanting to please people, I saw this issue of anger, and with the revelation another layer of forgiveness for him and myself. But in this matter of listening, he tried to warn me, to speak the truth. I simply chose not to pay attention.

As the days, weeks, and months continue, I'm still learning my identity and my ancestral background.

———◆———

Questions to Challenge You

1. Do you have any addictions? If so, be honest with yourself and name them?
   Note: These do not have to be drugs, alcohol, sex or anything like that. It can be an addiction to fru-fru coffee, chocolate or sugar, television, etc. Addiction can be anything you use in life as an attempt to fill a God hole.

2. Are you willing to do whatever it takes to overcome addictions that cause harm to yourself or others?

3. What steps will you take to overcome an addiction?
   Hint: The first step might be praying for revelation and then admitting to whatever God shows you.

Chapter 7~Skeptical

"*Truth is like the sun. You can shut it out for a time, but it ain't going away.*"

~Elvis Presley

ALL MY LIFE, PEOPLE told me I'm too friendly.

I'm not sure how anyone can be too friendly, especially in a world where most people look out only for themselves. But I can admit it. I am.

Some people are very skeptical about who they let into their circle because of the hurt and fears they dealt with in the past. Honestly, I don't blame them. We have good reasons to take precautions with our heart. King Solomon, who lived in 970-930 B.C., offered instruction and his wisdom by writing the book of Proverbs. He said, "Guard your heart above all else, for it is the source of life" (Proverbs 4:23 CSB).

While I have no problem with friendliness, letting people into my inner circle of confidence requires a discernment. I can show friendship without letting down my guard and allowing people to get too close too soon. That's simply wisdom. To guard our hearts, we must protect it against those who wish to do harm.

Learning my daddy fathered so many children caused skepticism. As a single woman, not knowing all my family members, I grew more skeptical. I dated one guy for a while. Then, a few years after we broke up, I discovered a possibility we are distant cousins.

That hurt me. I'm thankful we don't have a close blood relationship. Still, I realized we could have been close cousins, not distant ones.

I had to encourage myself. "Teresa, don't trip! You didn't know, and y'all ain't getting back together. No way."

I met a dude with the last name of Carpenter. I told him, "I'm related to Carpenters. That's my dad's last name."

He said his family is not from Texas.

I told him my family comes from all over the world.

Later, he asked how I felt about dating him.

Nice man, and I wouldn't mind dating him—maybe. I didn't know him well enough to say yes, but I had a level of interest. So, I said, "We can see." Anxiety popped up. "Whoa, whoa, whoa. Before we go any further, I wanna take a DNA test, because I don't wanna fall in love with you and later down the line find out we're related."

He agreed at first. Then, when it was time to take the test, he didn't want to. He tried to assure me. "We're not related."

"Well, I don't wanna date you. If we don't have 100% certainty we're not related, I won't go there."

I didn't know whether he might be a relative because my daddy had all those kids. The not knowing frightened me.

You can bet I'm more skeptical and mature now about who and what I let in my circle. I might still be too friendly, but only to a point. I trust those closest to me, and if I can't trust someone, they don't join my circle.

Some people only want to connect when they see what level I'm on and who I know to make them look good. If they don't see how I can make their life better without giving in return, they have no interest in me. It took me a minute to learn that one, and a few painful lessons with a few I let enter my circle. Discovering the truth about them broke my heart, because I thought they cared about me, not what I could do to better them. When they couldn't get what they wanted, I saw the true side of them arise. A painful lesson that taught me to guard my heart more.

Unfortunately, some people come around and want to be involved in your life, but if they feel you ain't got no money, they don't wanna fool with ya. I learned that lesson after many times of God trying to teach me. He finally got through, and revealed how I did that so often in my past, healing me from the pain and the need to let that kind of person get in my circle.

My daddy, Hot Shot, taught me one thing. You ain't never gotta look like what you got. I have a kind heart, but I peep game. Sometimes, I found myself being too kind to the wrong people. When they took advantage of me, that was my fault.

Now, I pray about relationships—especially if I feel a check in my spirit about someone.

Of course, it hurts to reject people. I had to learn rejection equals protection, no matter what a person or relationship means to you or how long you been knowing them. Years of knowing a person doesn't always mean you "know" him or her. We spend time with a host of people without fully knowing them. We can't read minds or hearts, and anyone can put on a good show for a time.

For someone addicted to people pleasing, the act of rejection came even harder. If I had to break off a relationship, I didn't please them. If I said no to someone who wanted to use me, I didn't please him or her. And if I didn't give them what they wanted or needed, I let those friends down.

When I realized unhealthy relationships hurt my heart, God helped me let go of those toxic situations and broke me from that need to always please. Not easy, but as time passes, I am better about never entering some of those associations.

In the same way I don't want to date a relative, I don't want to let a person into my circle who will hurt me. I listen to the Holy Spirit and guard my heart—a process I continue working to achieve.

To those who hurt me, I forgive you. That's for me, not for you. Just because I forgive you, I don't have to deal with you. Forgiveness never means I knowingly let a person inside my circle to continue hurting me.

Now I pray God connects me to the right people and teaches me how to receive them and enjoy healthy relationships. If I seem a bit too skeptical, I'm okay with that. My heart deserves guarding.

Questions to Challenge You

1. How do you feel about DNA testing?

2. Would you willingly submit to DNA testing?

3. What excites or frightens you about having your DNA tested and perhaps learning secrets about your family?

Chapter 8~My DNA Summary Ethnicity Estimates

"I believe that unarmed truth and unconditional love will have the final word in reality. This is why right, temporarily defeated, is stronger than evil triumphant."

~Martin Luther King, Jr.

---❧---

WHEN DNA RESULTS CAME back, I found out all my
family consists of much more than African American
ancestors. We are Cameroon, Congo, and Western Bantu
Peoples, Nigerian, Mali Benin and Togo Ivory Coast, and
Ghana, Ireland, Senegal, Norway, England and North-
western Europe, Southern Bantu Peoples, Indigenous
Americans, and North Wells.

Communities where my bloodline lived included Early Virginia African Americans, Early North Carolina,
East Texas, Arkansas and Louisiana African American. It
might be a lot more. I had no idea about any of this.

As I reviewed the information before me, God revealed
I still had a lot of unforgiveness in my heart toward people
that hurt me by saying Mama didn't know who my daddy
was. Every mama ought to know who got her pregnant,
or at least have some idea. Sometimes people know, but
they won't say.

Of course, I had to cry out to God and ask Him to
teach me how to forgive those people, alongside my mama
and daddy. I read Mark 11:24-26. "Therefore, I say unto
you, what things soever ye desire, when ye pray, believe
that ye receive them, and ye shall have them. And when
ye stand praying, forgive, if ye have ought against any:
that your Father also which is in heaven may forgive you
your trespasses. But if ye do not forgive, neither will your
Father which is in heaven forgive your trespasses."

It's not easy to forgive people that hurt you. Honestly, sometimes, you don't want to forgive them. Admit it. We all have those people we just want to see judged for the way they hurt, used, or abused us. Many times, we need to ask the Lord to make us want to forgive, even if we aren't quite ready. And Lord knows I had plenty of sin for Him to forgive, so I had to pardon those who hurt me.

Imagine asking God to forgive you for your sins and God says, "Heck no, because you won't forgive others for what they did to you."

Let me encourage you to forgive your enemies. Holding the past against someone else does not hurt them—holding unforgiveness only hurts yourself. It takes time and often repeated forgiveness. I can't say I do this all the time, but I keep trying.

As Paul the Apostle said, "Brethren, I count not myself to have apprehended: but this one thing I do, forgetting those things which are behind, and reaching forth unto those things which are before, I press toward the mark for the prize of the high calling of God in Christ Jesus" (Philippians 3:13-14).

I started listening to gospel music by people such as Donald Lawrence and Le'Andria Johnson. "Deliver Me (This is My Exodus)" really blessed my soul during this difficult time of battling with unforgiveness.

After the DNA testing, I must admit to going on Ancestry.com to build my family tree. Although difficult finding out who you are, I needed to know the truth—wanted to see my relatives. Then, I had to realize God works in mysterious ways.

I found people I was related to but never knew. On Ancestry, I could see both my mom's and dad's sides, filled with ancestors others discovered before I joined. On one side of my family, I discovered unknown biological relationships with some people. That's when God exposed truth to me. I still had unforgiveness and hatred in my heart.

So hard to let go, but I cried out to God for His help. I wanted to know why God allowed me to go through all the things I endured.

As I mentioned earlier, people always told me I had a Joseph anointing on my life. If you read Joseph's story (Genesis 37-50), he did not have an easy anointed bringing family together, getting to know who you are. In fact, his brothers hated him enough to sell him into slavery.

Joseph had every right to harbor anger and unforgiveness against his brothers, but he understood something very important. God used what his brothers meant for evil for good—to save nations.

I've been through so many things in life. I get exhausted going through all this. Dealing with past pain doesn't come without an emotional price. But unforgiveness destroys you. Yes, a hard battle to fight and win, it is not easy to forgive someone.

Then, with all this DNA discovery going on, it made me not even want to be related to anyone. I didn't want to tell anybody my discoveries about all our relatives. I battled hard, enduring the process of opening my heart and dealing with layers of emotions—some things I thought I had already conquered.

Eventually, I had to let go and let God heal me. Everybody didn't do to me what my past did to me. If I don't forgive other people for what they did to me and for who they are, then I have no effect on them, but I'm affecting myself—and not in a positive way.

Questions to Challenge You

1. If you tested your DNA and learned something unexpected, how do you think you might react?

2. What would be the worst thing you could discover through DNA testing results?

3. What would be the best think you could discover through DNA testing results?

Chapter 9~Still Not Relieved

"Is there no balm in Gilead; is there no physician there? why then is not the health of the daughter of my people recovered?"
Prophet Jeremiah, Jeremiah 8:22

———— ❧ ————

As MENTIONED, I GREW up hearing, "You don't got no daddy." That came from Mama.

Others said, "Your mama don't know who your daddy is." Words like these stick in a young girl's mind, leaving behind confusion, frustration, pain, and downright anger.

I remember asking Mama why she didn't give me my daddy's last name. She always responded the same way. "When you grown, you get married and change your own last name."

Those calloused responses left wounds, some of which needed healing. Even after the Lord healed me, such a deep level of wounding leaves scars, and the slightest touch can bring renewed pain. Words, events, movies, songs, and many things can touch that scar and send me to the floor in pain. I learned to deal with those unexpected moments, so they no longer defeat me.

While many people unintentionally hurt my heart, some people answered that burning question about my daddy. But for some reason, I ignored all the times people said, "Girl, you look just like Hot Shot."

I often wondered if Daddy was pregnant with me or Mama. That alone should have convinced me of my daddy's identity, yet I continued seeking answers.

As Mama aged, her health declined, and she went to live in a nursing home. After struggling through a healing process, I made a gut-wrenching decision. Based on biblical principles, I opted to honor her regardless of the many hurts in the past. I read and reread Exodus 20:12. "Honor thy father and thy mother: that thy days may be long upon the land which the Lord thy God giveth thee."

Unfortunately, doing my best to obey this one of the Ten Commandments tried my faith. Without God's grace, I couldn't. But He kept reminding me, and I continued caring for her.

One day, I again faced a person who said my mama didn't know who my daddy was. The words tore at my heart scars, so I went to visit Mama that week.

I again asked, "Who's my daddy?

"Girl, get out of my face." Her response shocked me, so I took a deep breath, praying for the truth.

"No, Mama. Who is my daddy?"

"Out of all these years, you don't know who your daddy is?"

I pushed down the frustration. "No, Mama. Please. Who is my daddy?"

Her face didn't flinch. "Girl, yo' daddy name Dick, and everybody else daddy name Dick, cause that's what help get you here. Now get the hell out of my face."

Now that cracked me up. I couldn't help laughing out loud. Mama didn't laugh. She meant what she said with all seriousness. At the moment, humor took over, and I couldn't resist it.

For a moment, relief flooded over me. Sometimes laughter does that. Short-lived, I wasn't relieved. I wondered if I would ever know the full sense of relief—if I could ever know the truth and find release from all the questions.

About the time I think I'm there, here comes another situation.

This dude was trying to bash my daddy, saying all sorts of negative crap. I almost bashed him right back. Holy Spirit must've been working overtime that day, because I didn't. I was finna' change my last name to Carpenter after my daddy. And despite anything he did or didn't do, no one gonna get away with putting my daddy down. After all those years of wondering, I found out the truth, and I sure didn't want some dude telling me only worthless junk about Daddy.

Thankfully, God connected me with wise people that sat me down, encouraged me, and gave me a new perspective.

Many said, "Teresa, your name is already popular, and some people are jealous of you. Just keep that name as your stage name."

Their words made sense. I grasped the possibility of why some people spoke hurtful words in connection with my name. Although I always wanted my daddy's last name, changing it at that point in life meant a ton of work.

Plus, if I changed my name legally, would I lose ground I gained as an author, actor, and minister? Would people know me by a different name? I worked hard to get my name out there, and I wasn't ready to give it up. As much as I wanted to go by my daddy's last name, I didn't want to lose the accomplishments I made under the name of Teresa Tarpley.

I let it go and kept my name. While I still lacked complete relief, a sense of peace worked its way into my life. At least I knew the truth, and I could live with that, despite my last name.

Then God spoke to me and promised I will soon be married, and then my name will change. Lord knows I can't wait.

Now, if I could just figure out what soon means.

Questions to Challenge You

1. If you could make one wish, knowing it would come true, what would you wish?

2. Have you ever wanted to be someone else? Live a different life? Have a different name? Go somewhere far away?

3. Dreams or visions become goals and goals become tasks that fulfill those dreams. Think about one thing you dream. Can you make it a reality? Why or why not? If you could, would you change something drastically in your life to reach that dream?

Chapter 10~What A Relief

"And ye shall know the truth, and the truth shall make you free."

Jesus Christ, John 8:32

EVEN THOUGH PEOPLE TOLD me I look just like my daddy, looks can be deceiving. Before I knew the truth, I didn't want to base anything on looks alone.

But if he was telling the truth, I wanted to know my family—especially my brothers and sisters.

Well, I met a lady that knew my daddy. She told me about a cousin that lives outside the state of Texas where I live. I talked to him, and we exchanged numbers.

Although we never met each other in person, we talk on the phone all the time. We also became social media friends to keep up with each other. His acceptance of me as a cousin started the process of finding family members and gave me the courage to try.

If Hot Shot told the truth, I had brothers, sisters, nieces and nephews, and perhaps a long list of distant relatives. The thought made my head spin, but I needed to know.

In 2020, I finally stepped out in faith and got on Ances try.com. From my first time on the site, I started learning a lot. DNA doesn't lie. Anxiety pressed down on me. What if I didn't match the family I believed was mine? What if my DNA matched no one? I waited—not necessarily patiently, knowing I couldn't rush any of it. Tempted to give in to fear, I prayed for peace and to trust the Lord with the results.

August became a challenging month for me years ago. My daddy passed Aug 1, 2007. His birthday was Aug 24th. Then Mama passed on Aug 22, 2016. As August 2022 approached, I grieved for my parents more than ever. With unanswered questions, the pain of their absence grew more intense. The month brought sorrow, loneliness, and depression.

Well, guess what? During that time of intense grieving, my cousin who lives outside Texas called and said our DNA results matched.

I finally breathed deeply, relieved to know Hot Shot was, in fact, my daddy.

Tarpley may be my legal last name, but Carpenter is my bloodline.

Relief poured over me while I talked with my cousin, finally knowing Hot Shot was my daddy.

Ancestry pairs DNA matches, and the more people join, the more relatives you may find.

I'm sick of the traditional crap. Just because you look like someone doesn't mean you're blood related. After the way I grew up, I thank God for truth and for the technology that can answer questions for those who don't know their father's identity. I'm not alone in that. Unfortunately, the age of sleeping around left many kids wondering about their blood relatives.

I'm 53 years old and feel so relieved to know finally 100% that Hot Shot is my daddy. Like the old Alka-Seltzer "plop, plop, fizz, fizz, oh what a relief it is," the constant knots and anxiety in my gut disappeared with the truth.

Let me encourage you. As long as you're living, you're never too old to do what you wanna do. If you need answers to your ancestors, ask questions of those you know. And if you must seek DNA evidence, do it. It may not turn out as you expected, but at least you know the truth.

Despite the situation, I no longer blame my parents. Perhaps that statement proves I matured and learned to forgive them. I'll never know what they went through to make them do the things they did, but I learned from them the dos and don'ts of life. They taught me without trying. Because of what I went through as a child and even into adulthood, I know how deeply my actions affect my children and everyone in my life.

I thank God for Mama and Daddy as my parents. Since meeting many of his relatives, I truly love my Carpenter family. They accepted me with loving, open arms as part of their family, and for that, I cannot express enough gratitude.

Even though I wanted to change my last name to the Carpenter name, I think about Naomi in the book of Ruth.

If you never read the story found in the book of Ruth, take a minute to read the four brief chapters in the Bible. It shows a beautiful relationship between two women who became family by marriage but lasted because of a heart connection.

The story opens with Naomi in a foreign land, where she lost her husband and both of her sons. In biblical times, a woman didn't just go get a job to provide for herself. Although she loved her daughters-in-law, she told them to go home to their fathers and perhaps find new husbands.

Returning to her home town of Bethlehem, Naomi wanted to change her name to Mara (which in Hebrew means bitter). She didn't think her birth name represented her any longer. With a shadow hanging over her head, Naomi felt anything but pleasant. At the end of the story, we find Naomi happy again.

Because of her, Ruth (the daughter-in-law who stuck by Naomi) not only found a good husband, but had a son Naomi adored. As a side note, we later see Ruth in the lineage of Jesus. (See Ruth 1-4 and Matthew 1:5-6.)

Like Naomi, I had to learn who God says I am. My name couldn't change my life any more than Naomi could change her name to fit her current emotions. God created her to be pleasant and bless the people surrounding her, even though, for a time, she was bitter.

I can admit it—so was I. Just keeping it real. I always hated my last name and desperately wanted my dad's name, Carpenter.

But who God sees when He looks at me doesn't matter what name anyone calls me. Whether I use Tarpley or Carpenter, I am the same Teresa.

I'm amazed by the way God sees people. Throughout Scripture, we can find examples of His view over how others view us or even how we view ourselves.

Gideon—hiding in a winepress, terrified of the Midianites. Gideon means warrior, and the angel called him a valiant warrior. Not just warrior, but a brave, honorable one. (See Judges 6:11-12.)

In Matthew 16:17-18, Jesus changed Simon's name (hearing) to Peter (rock). What God saw when he looked at the brash young disciple differed from what others saw.

Where most saw David as a shepherd boy, God saw a king. (See 1 Samuel 16:5-13.) God also called David a man after his own heart, even though he fell into temptation and sinned. (See 1 Samuel 13:14 and Acts 13:22.)

These are only a few examples of how God sees something we never imagine in others or ourselves. "For the LORD seeth not as man seeth; for man looketh on the outward appearance, but the LORD looketh on the heart" (1 Samuel 16:7b).

Regardless of my name, God created me with a purpose. As relieved as I felt to learn the truth about Daddy, I am far

more grateful my Heavenly Father knows my name—and
all he planned for me.

Questions to Challenge You

1. How do you see yourself?

2. How do other people see you? Is it different from
   how you view yourself?

3. How does God see you? If you don't know, ask
   Him. Does his view differ from your self-percep-
   tion and that of others?

Chapter 11~Got to Be Real

"*Anything will give up its secrets if you love it enough. Not only have I found that when I talk to the little flower or to the little peanut they will give up their secrets, but I have found that when I silently commune with people, they give up their secrets also—if you love them enough.*"

George Washington Carver

———— ❊ ————

IT'S TIME TO STOP holding back deep, dark family se-crets. All that old junk, "what goes on in this house stays in this house," needs to disappear.

Again, I'm letting it out. It's time to be real and start having family reunions. Stop all that clique junk. Even if you have an issue with someone, it is time to stop holding back secrets. Tell your children and other family members who they are related to. Don't wait until someone dies to connect with relatives. I'm sick of funeral reunions and refuse to attend those any longer. Yes, we attend funerals to pay our respects to the deceased person, but why do people expect relatives to show up for a funeral when they knew nothing about that person or anyone else there? Nope. No more funeral reunions for this girl. I want to know my relatives now, before one of them passes away.

I must admit it's painful not knowing all my family. I missed out on wonderful relationships because I didn't know we had the same bloodline. When I find out about a connection I didn't know before, I tell everybody. While on social media, I may receive comments from two friends who have no clue about their blood relationship. And I make sure to tell them. We need to know this information for a multitude of reasons.

Now, just because common blood flows through our veins doesn't mean I have to deal with you. Bloodlines don't always put us with the best people in the world. Just about every family has a scoundrel somewhere in the past—or maybe the present and future. Nevertheless, I wanna know my family. Many people call me cousin although we have none of the same bloodlines. I call them cousins by heart.

Some people may not want the truth to come out. Oh well, I don't care. If you are looking for your family, don't let what someone thinks discourage you. Yes, it can embarrass people when indiscretions come out. Touchy subject because we all make mistakes. But those hidden secrets can prove devastating, as we discussed early in this book. As DNA technology improves and more people take the test, truth will come out. After my testing, a man found me on social media. He found me as a match and wanted to connect.

Long before all the DNA stuff, I met a man who stayed at the same nursing home as my mom. He was her cousin, and I had no idea. He named off several people—relatives I didn't know carried my same blood. Eventually, I'll dig deeper in my mom's family history and discover unknown blood relatives there, too.

Keep in mind, the last name you go by has nothing to do with determining bloodlines. I have neither my mother's or father's last name, and both of them left this earth years ago. That doesn't make me any less a family member. I'm still the daughter of one man and one woman, and the blood flowing through my veins matches to many other people. We all need to know those connections. Although a last name gives you a place to start, don't get trapped thinking you aren't related just because you have a different one than your parents or other family members.

My biological last names are Boozer and Carpenter. Please feel free to reach out to me. I'm still looking for all my family, especially my brothers and sisters. More than knowing about you, I want to connect and possibly form a relationship to whatever level we both desire.

People might try to tell you many people share the same uncommon or common last name. Very true. The same or a similar last name does not guarantee you belong to the same bloodline, but it gives you a place to start.

Whether two people have the same or different last names matters little. No one knew me as a Carpenter for most of my life. A DNA test tells it all. I ain't going off no one else's opinion. I'll see for myself. And yes, I will share what I find, because we all need to know our families.

The popularity of Ancestry and other programs proves humans want to know about those who came before us and those who share the same blood with us today.

As this technology grows and becomes more accessible at lower costs, don't be surprised if an unknown relative pops up. You hear stories of this every day, so don't think staying off Ancestry protects you from someone finding you. The links and lines flow freely, and whether you want truth out there, it shows up.

You can try to deny a connection—trust me, I didn't want to find some people in my bloodline. But DNA tells a story, and you can't deny it.

Wow! I have a lot of stepmoms thanks to Daddy. I didn't know how any of them might react to me. When I started meeting them, they showed me a lot of love. It's funny, not ha-ha funny but ironic funny, because I'm closer to family I'm just meeting than the ones I knew all my life. Even the ladies my dad dated but didn't have children together openly accepted me. We may not be blood but still consider each other as brothers and sisters, aunts, uncles, nieces and nephews. To think I had all these relatives I never knew. My sadness turned to joy.

Perhaps that's why I want everything out in the open. If I found joy, maybe others in my family can, too. And if I encourage people outside of my blood to seek truth, I hope they find joy like I did.

Sadly, not every story ends well. DNA also reveals the identity of decades old crimes, serial killers and rapists, and scoundrels that want nothing to do with the vast number of children they abandoned. You hear those stories, too.

We take a risk of finding out truth we wish we didn't know. Even if that happens, wouldn't you rather learn now, before some big mess?

To parents, grandparents, anyone who has family ties. Some of you know the secrets. You kept them hidden for years. Be gracious and stop hiding the darkness.

Jesus said, "And ye shall know the truth, and the truth shall make you free (John 8:32). When the truth comes into the light, it frees us. All those dark secrets keep us in bondage, eating away at our souls. And they often affect generations after us, who do not know why their life feels so messed up.

The sins of one generation may remain hidden for decades even, but not without consequences. And eventually, those secrets come out. What happens in the dark will one day shine for everyone to see. In the meantime, people end up deeply wounded because of those secrets.

For those left in the wake of the hidden, keep your head up. Remember, you have a choice to change what you don't know.

May be the peace of God guide you to expose the things that keep you in bondage. As you travel a journey of discovery, be sure to forgive—no matter how difficult it seems. Bathe your search with prayer and the wisdom and encouragement of those you trust as you seek to say *Everything's Out in the Open.*

Questions to Challenge You

1. When others look at you, do they see the authentic you or someone you want to portray for others?

2. How willing are you to share the secrets of your life?
   Note: Not everyone needs to know every secret you keep. Some secrets need exposure to light to overcome them, though. These are secrets you can consider sharing with those closest to you, acquaintances, and the general public. With God's guidance, determine which belong to each of these groups.

3. What do you fear most about letting others see the real you?

About the Author

TFounder/CEO of Hurt, Broken, Now Healed and Delivered Ministries, Teresa Tarpley released her first book in 2016, *HeartBroken: Now Healed and Delivered*. In ministering to other people, Teresa focuses on those coming out of addiction and striving to live a new life with Jesus as their guide.

In 2017, Teresa became a radio talk show host of *Straight Up Radio Talk Show*. Based on her life story, she launched the stage play *I am Beautiful* as the executive producer. Teresa also played a part in the stage play, which opened doors for several minor roles in movies. She became a certified actress.

Recognized for the best stage play executive producer during 2019 in Phoenix, Arizona, Teresa enjoys acting, hoping each role she plays ministers to someone. In addition, she shares her testimony whenever the opportunity arises.

Following the release of her second book in 2021, Teresa continued writing and releasing other books while working as a Certified Nurse Aid, auditioning for parts in various movies, becoming a stand-up comedian, and searching for her family ancestry.

All her books are available at discounted prices for bulk purchases, sales promotions, fund-raising events, or for educational purchases.

For more information about the author, to obtain special pricing or to schedule Teresa as a speaker for your event, please contact Teresa Tarpley by phone or email.

PO Box 50162
Fort Worth, TX 76105
(817) 210-7517
Email: minister.ttarpley@yahoo.com

Other Books By Teresa Tarpley

HeartBroken: Now Healed and Delivered
ISBN: 978-0692583739
Radical Women, 2016

———— ⚜ ————

Why Y'all Treat Me So Bad?
ISNB: 978-1734039832
Radical Women, 2021

———— ⚜ ————

Mother of Inmates
ISBN: 978-1734039863
Radical Women, 2021

Ain't No Future in the Back
ISBN: 978-1734039887
Radical Women, 2022

Coming Soon from Teresa Tarpley

Withdrawals
ISBN: 9798988648505
Radical Women, 2023
Target release date by August 2023

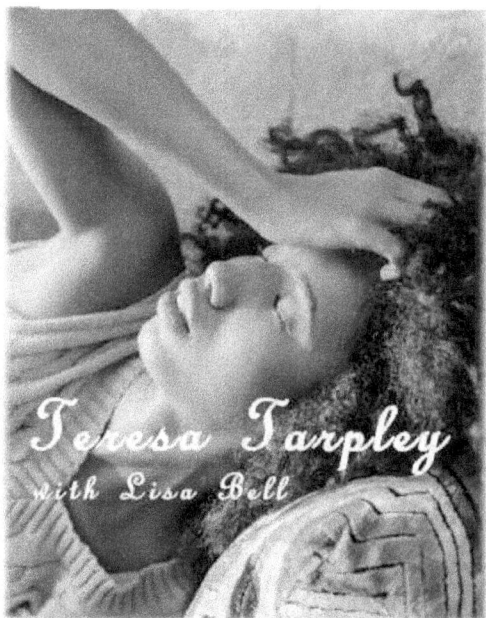

Withdrawals

Teresa Tarpley
with Lisa Bell

Coming Soon

About Radical Women

Owner of Radical Women, Lisa Bell, lives in Granbury, Texas. She retired early in 2023 from her position as an editor for NOW Magazines, LLC, covering two of nine markets. She still offers freelance editing of all types (including developmental editing), interior design, custom cover creation, and she strives to guide and assist writers in publishing their stories independently or with traditional publishers. Whether fiction or non-fiction, Lisa has experience and knowledge to make a good story great.

Lisa also serves as a coach for two writing groups under the name of Radical Writers. She strives to teach writers the skills of writing so their work becomes the best they can achieve. Through writing groups, individual coaching, editing and more, she takes pride in finished products that rival any book regardless of the publisher.

Lisa has published hundreds of articles and multiple books. To learn more about Lisa, contact her by phone, text, email, or visiting the bylisabell website.

www.bylisabell.com.
(817) 269-9066
lisabell@bylisabell.com
www.texasradicalwriters.com